VOLKSWAGEN
BUS
CAMPER, VAN & PICK-UP
Colour Family Album

FREEDOM IS - A VW BUS

This book is dedicated to Gladys Barnes, with our love.

Other books of interest to enthusiasts and available from Veloce -

First published in 1997 by Veloce Publishing Plc.,33, Trinity Street, Dorchester, Dorset DT1 1TT, England. Fax: 01305 268864.

ISBN 1 874105 78 2
UPC 36847-00078-3

Throughout this book logos, model names and designations, etc., may have been used for the purposes of identification, illustration and decoration. Such names are the property of the trademark holder as this is not an official publication.

Readers with ideas for automotive books, or books on other transport or related hobby subjects, are invited to write to Veloce Publishing at the above address.

British Library Cataloguing in Publication Data -
A catalogue record for this book is available from the British Library.

Typesetting (Avant Garde), design and page make-up all by Veloce on AppleMac.

Printed in Hong Kong.

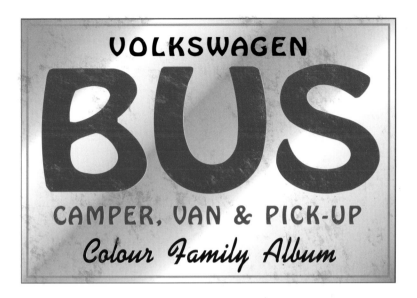

ANDREA & DAVID SPARROW

VELOCE PUBLISHING PLC
PUBLISHERS OF FINE AUTOMOTIVE BOOKS

THANKS

Very special thanks to David Eccles and Terry Ellis of the Split-Screen Club: an organisation dedicated to the preservation and restoration of Type 2 Volkswagens and to getting together people who are enthusiastic about the VW Bus in all its forms. Thanks, too, to Jochen and Roswitha Brauer of the famous Bullikartei, Jos and Lieve Quets of the Limburgse Kever Club, Buzz and his long-suffering mother, Marc Maskery, Louise Berrisford, Guy Robertson, Ricky James, Chris Hull, Robin Allen, Gerald Wilke of the Kever Club Netherlands, Karsten Kleinwachter,

Helga Bitterling, Hartmut Thun, Carsten Rehage, Bernd-Dietrich Eiteneier, Arne Reckermann, Rudiger Stegmiller, Tina Tepe, Kelsey Walker, Wehner Heinz, Mathilda Celie, John Dieleman, Paul Harrison, Bea Vrancken, Sabine Lyket, Raoul Verbeeman, Michael Irlensbusch, Francois Beyens, Paul Hamilton of the Surrey Owners' Club, Etienne Mertens, Dirk Grobben, Mon and Cory Martens, Peter Valentin, Martine and Marc Plaetsier, Jade Bond, Dave Simmons, Louis and Sandy

Pelham, Wolfgang Staib, Frank Samson of the Belgian VW Kever Club, Koen De Smet, Berthold Krupp, Wehrfuhrer Feiwilligen Fuerwehr Altenahr, Rodney MacDonald, Marc Meulemans, Fazio Lepine, Klas Treude, Hechthild Girsig, Dave Chappell of Trevelgue Holiday Park (site of the now famous "Run to the Sun"), Dimitrie and Marie-France Urbain (a big thankyou for all the information, especially on Westfalia). Special thanks to Yannick Boes, Director of Cristal Beer, Alken, Belgium, for the use of his fire truck and premises and to Samantha Smith of the British Ports Authority.

CONTENTS

INTRODUCTION

There are few motor car manufacturers that can lay claim to a success story like that of the Volkswagen Beetle. There are even less that can boast two such stories. Yet the second Volkswagen model - known variously as the Type 2, the Transporter, the Bus and the Bulli - made quite a name for itself over its thirty-plus years of production.

Now approaching its half-century, the Type 2 in all its forms still commands respect for its ruggedness, longevity and versatility, and has many thousands of fans all over the world. Some are also Beetle fanatics. Some have a particular interest in the earlier Split-window examples, or in the later Bay-windows. The last of the Transporters - the

Wedge - commands a following, too.

The beauty of the Transporter was that it could be so many things - delivery van, minibus, camper, or a mixture of all of them. Like the Beetle, the Bus will be around for a long time to come.

Andrea Sparrow

1967 Split-window.

"A BOX ON WHEELS"

When Dr. Heinz Nordhoff took over as Managing Director of Volkswagen at Wolfsburg, in September 1949, he knew that he had an uphill task ahead of him. He'd been with the company just over eighteen months, appointed by the British authorities to head up the organisation when they handed control, which they'd exercised since the end of the war, back to Germany. Nordhoff knew that he had a first-class product in the Bee- tle, but he was also aware that the car's German nation- ality would count against it in some markets - its accept- ance around Europe was by no means assured. Still, Nordhoff needed foreign markets: he had to buy mod- ern machinery from other countries but the only way of paying for it was with foreign currency and the only way to get foreign currency was through exports. Nordhoff embarked on a huge export

The Transporter as a camper - starring for over forty years on campsites the world over. (Bay-window camper).

Cheers! The bus was a hit in the UK - and was especially popular with antipodean tourists, who would buy one in England for their European travels, and sell it again afterwards to another Aussie or Kiwi who would repeat the cycle. (1963 Split-window).

SLEEPING - CAR

Sleeping car, dining car, lounge car ... and it's a car too, of course! (1964 Split-window Dormobile camper).

drive, backing up the Beetle with a first-class sales, service and parts network. His plans worked; within the year he had quadrupled his export figures and doubled the factory's output.

Nordhoff's expansion plans for Wolfsburg were not based just around the Beetle. Almost as soon as he joined the company, he'd been told by his chief development engineer, Alfred Heasner, about plans to build a Volkswagen load-carrier. The original idea had come not from Heasner, but from Ben Pon, who had started importing Volkswagens to the Netherlands the previous year.

The Dutch Pon family business had had good relations with Germany for many years, importing German marques such as Opel. Pon was impressed by the work of Ferdinand Porsche, and discussions with the German authorities about the possibility of his importing their 'people's car' were well advanced - it had been agreed that the Netherlands should be the car's very first export market - when the war intervened and the discussions halted. Once the war was over, Pon was anxious to pursue the matter again and set about rebuilding a business relationship with Volkswagen. His opposite numbers in the negotiations

The Kombi's seats could not only be moved but could also be removed quickly and easily - van one minute, minibus the next. (Split-window Kombi).

this time were the officers in charge of the British zone. It was a tough time for all those trying to rebuild Germany's shattered infrastructure. The American and British zones were soon integrated, and in June 1946 the Americans set in motion a relief programme, called the Marshall Plan (after the American foreign secretary). By December, permission had been given for German businesses in the zone to start exporting their goods to Britain, the USA and the Netherlands ... the opportunity that Pon needed. Ben Pon visited both the Wolfsburg factory and the Minden-based economic headquarters of the British/American zone several times during the early part of 1947, and soon found himself appointed the official VW importer for the Netherlands.

It was during his visits to Wolfsburg that Ben Pon was struck by the suitability of the Volkswagen, in principle at least, for load-carrying. For easy movement of parts around the factory, some strange, but effective, trucks had been constructed out of Kubelwagen chassis. Although quite crude - and they had no need to be anything else - they performed admirably as load carriers. During a visit to Minden on 23rd April 1947, Pon did a quick sketch of how he envisaged a Volkswagen

The Transporter was nothing if not adaptable; it soon proved its worth with fire, police and ambulance services.
(Split-window fire engine).

The Transporter - especially in split-screen form - presented a friendly face to the world. (1951 Split-window with Beetle Cabriolet engine).

The perfect answer for freight - a box on wheels! Note the lack of separate indicator lights on this early panel van. (1956 Split-window Panel van).

"Let's see if Dad's got a big yellow steering wheel in his Bus."
(Split-window camper).

Small firms and big firms alike snapped up the Type 2 - the panel van version offered loads of advertising space, too!
(Split-window Panel van).

load-carrier would look. Colonel Charles Radclyffe, who was overseeing Wolfsburg at the time, was impressed, but confessed that he was unable to start on any new projects; the economic progress that was being made was astounding, but too much was at stake to risk a diverting venture, at least for the time being.

So the idea of a transporter had to wait until Heinz Nordhoff took over control at Wolfsburg before it could be taken seriously. So seriously did Nordhoff take it, though, that it was only a short while before the development department were set to work on the project. The first plans were ready and approved by the end of 1948, and the testing programme quickly began.

It soon became clear that the Beetle's chassis was not equal to the demands the team were placing on it. A rethink produced a new prototype - this time of monocoque construction with an additional subframe for extra support. Testing over long test track distances proved positive - Volkswagen's transporter would soon be a reality.

By May 1949, the development department was busy building four units for demonstration purposes, plus two different versions which would serve as prototypes for the

The Samba version of the Microbus - here taking on a Herbie theme - boasts 23 windows in all.
(Split-window Samba).

Transporter lovers finish their buses to the highest standard - whether restoring them to original condition, as here, or customising. (1965 Split-window Microbus).

VW's MPV for the 1990s, the Sharan.

Today's Type 2 customs range from mild to wild. Some have their roots in the California look (pages 20 & 21), others echo a flower power or Hippy theme (left). All reflect individual style.

Kombi/Minibus variations. There were many refinements to be attended to: although the transporter was designed as a practical and basic load-carrier, it was not intended to be crude. The heat from the engine was going to make the occupants very uncomfortable, so it was decided to enclose it more fully, which also had the advantage of making it quieter. The petrol filler, which had been located outside at the rear, was moved to inside the engine compartment; this, in turn, meant moving the spare wheel to a new site above the engine.

The first Volkswagen Transporter was introduced at a press conference on November 12th 1949, and went on sale to the public the following March. In essence, the production units looked very similar to the original design which Ben Pon had sketched in his notebook three years earlier, and they would continue to do so for many years to come. Nordhoff was not a man who believed in complicating matters for the sake of change; he'd had a very good product from the beginning, and he appreciated the fact.

The Type 2 Volkswagen (the Beetle was Type 1) was enthusiastically received from the start, both by the press and the public. It was soon clear that Volkswagen now had a second success story.

The story of their evolution is, for most vehicles, a catalogue of substantial redesign and revision until an optimum compromise is reached and then a totally new model is developed - usually within five or six years. The Volkswagen Transporter's story is of a very different nature. In over thirty years, there would be only two major milestones; with the exception of increases in engine size and power, the only other changes would be either small cosmetic and practical refinements, such as the replacement of semaphore arms with indicators, or responses to advances in technology, such as the introduction of a collapsible steering column. This is not to say that the Transporter was old-fashioned or stagnated, or that Volkswagen were stubborn in their attitude to it; it was simply a really good idea that worked well from the start!

Heinz Nordhoff was acknowledged by friends and critics alike to be a man of single-minded dedication to his ideals. His success at Volkswagen depended on his ability to forge the company's success quickly; the postwar years were no time for false starts and ponderous planning. When the Transporter idea was put to him, he acted on his convictions - he wanted it developed and in production as soon as possible. Nordhoff was a dynamic man, and enthusiastic to a degree which sometimes left his colleagues breathless. But, despite the formidable authority with which he ran proceedings at Wolfsburg, he was no tyrant. A family man with a great love of music, an accomplished artist and an experienced amateur photographer, he was often to be found deep in discussion with workers in the factory about their families and circumstances and the cultural life of the rapidly- growing town of Wolfsburg. He was mindful that the company needed to make money to grow and to succeed, not just for profits, but also to fulfil its responsibility to the workforce.

Many of today's major car manufacturers prefer to forget their early days and pioneering models. Requests for information on past events and models often fall on deaf ears. "We only make new motorcars with all the latest technology," seems to be quite a usual response. Yet, when Volkswagen launched the new Sharan MPV, they were more than happy to refer to their successful past; posters showed a Bus with typical 'sixties-style psychedelic paint-job alongside the new model, and VW's press information proudly reminded us that "Volkswagen defined the MPV with the launch, in 1950, of the Volkswagen Bus based on the Transporter." At that time the Transporter was unique. Nordhoff himself put his finger on the reason for its popularity when he said that "When what you need is a box on wheels, then the perfect answer is ... a box on wheels!"

SPLIT-WINDOW

The first Transporters came in panel van form. The bodywork was quite austere: a perfect illustration of the adage that form follows function. Access to the loadspace was via doors in the side - and the volume of that loadspace was 162 cubic feet (4.58 cubic metres) - quite remarkable for a vehicle of such modest external dimensions. Early customers soon discovered two major advantages of the new VW: it could swallow vast loads with ease and, weighing in at just 975kg (2150lb), it had a load capacity of 750kg (1653lb).

The van was very well balanced on the road, too, regardless of how much load it was carrying. The weight of cab and driver over the front axle balanced beautifully the weight of the engine over the rear, with load-weight between the two. Although not the speediest or most powerful of vehicles, the Transporter's 1131cc engine gave 25bhp, and it could manage a maximum speed of just over 56mph (90kph). There was something special about the new VW - although designed as a purely practical box-on-

wheels with very little in the way of bright-work or other embellishment, nonetheless the Transporter had a very definite and unique character. Possibly because the split windscreen and curved front with central VW roundel gave it a 'face,' and because it was just so useful, it easily became a trusted and well-liked companion.

It was just two months before the first variation on the theme appeared, in the shape of the Kombi. This had side windows, and removable seats in the load area, making it extremely adaptable; ideal as a working van in the week, it could become a people carrier/car again at a moment's notice. The following month the Microbus was launched. This was available as a seven, eight or nine-seater, and had a higher level of interior trim than the Kombi, including a full-width dash-board. This trio of Panel van, Kombi and Microbus brought to fruition all the hard work, testing and trials that had been undertaken with the prototypes prior to the launch. Their success was immediate and, by the end of the year,

The engine from a 1954 Beetle Cabriolet has been fitted to this 1951 bus. It provides 30bhp - perhaps less than ideal for the owner's Alpine Touring ...

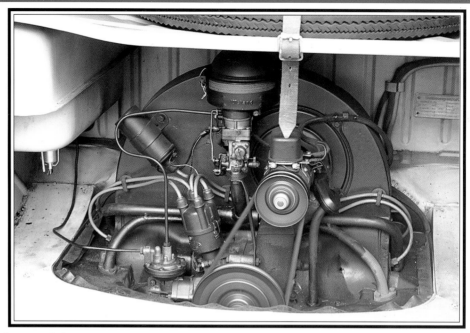

The VW always delivers - whether you live in town or in the sticks.
(1951 Split-window Microbus).

the daily tally of Type 2s rolling off the production line at Wolfsburg was around sixty.

A special version of the Microbus appeared in 1951. This was the Samba, which boasted extra windows at the rear corners giving a startling window tally of twenty-three in all! In September 1952, Volkswagen introduced a Pick-up version of the Type 2. It was an obvious extension to the Transporter range, which would further broaden the customer base, although a certain amount of reposition-ing of mechanical compo-nents had to be done to make the Pick-up arrange-ment work. The fuel tank found a new home further forward, over the gearbox now rather than over the engine. The spare wheel, meanwhile, was re-sited behind the locker which was under the platform and accessed from the side.

For 1954, the Transporter got a larger engine of 1192cc, which increased the power to 30bhp. Another important development that year was the introduction of the right-hand-drive option, and the 100,000th Transporter was completed at Wolfsburg.

There were major changes afoot during 1955. The chassis was strengthened, and the size of the wheels reduced. The Pick-up's fuel-tank posi-tioning was adopted across the whole Type 2 range; this enabled the huge rear "barn door" to be replaced with a smaller engine access door and a hatch door for access to the rear interior of the vehicle. The spare wheel was

The 18.55 VW from Altenahr leaves from platform 1. (1965 Split-window Microbus).

Faithful companion. The functional Transporter's load-carrying capacity was phenominal and its ruggedness and reliability endeared it to many thousands of users around the world. (1956 Split-window Panel van).

repositioned behind the front seat, and all models took onboard the Microbus's full-width dashboard. A new ventilation system was introduced, resulting in the fitting of intake grilles over the front windscreens. In essence, the range had been modernised in line with the less austere thinking of the mid-'fifties: the war had been over for a decade and, although times were still hard, there was no longer quite such a need for bare minimalism.

1956 was a special year for the Transporter. Both Bus and Beetle were selling well, the millionth Beetle having left the production line in August the previous year. Production was on the increase, and space was at a premium at Wolfsburg so Volkswagen decided to end Transporter production there and transfer it, lock, stock and barrel, to a purpose-built factory in Hanover. The new facility would have the capacity to build 250 units per day, using state of the art technology and providing first class training and facilities for staff.

It was 1958 before any further changes were made. In this year, the Double Crew Cab was introduced. It was an ideal vehicle for a group of workers needing to carry tools, materials and so on, but also preferring to travel 'indoors' themselves! The cab seated six, but still left plenty of room for equipment in the load areas. A more powerful engine was introduced across the range that year, too; it was of the same capacity, but

Water has its uses, of course, but air-cooling ensured that the Bus, like its sibling the Beetle, kept on going in all conditions. (Split-window Kombi).

Inside the Samba, there's plenty of room to stetch out - and plenty of windows to look out through.

Herbie-liveried Samba with Safari windows open - definitely a winner.

The Cal-look, so popular with Beetle owners, has influenced Bus-lovers, too ...

*Two ways to raise the roof - a high-top and concertina roof provide standing room.
(High-top and Dormobile Split-window campers).*

its increased compression ratio gave an extra 4bhp. Improvements to the gearbox, which extended the influence of synchromesh to first gear, were also introduced across the range in 1958. In the cosmetic department, the bumpers were made bigger, and the brake light was combined with the main clusters instead of being isolated in the middle. To comply with regulations in force in the USA, American-spec bumpers with bull-bar and over-riders were introduced as an option.

A decade of Transporter production was celebrated in March 1960. Changes to the Bus included saying goodbye to old-fashioned semaphore arm direction indicators in favour of modern flashing indicator lights - incorporated into the cluster at the rear, but fitted on little '59 Cadillac-style pods at the front. The one millionth Transporter unit rolled off the production line in August 1961. Ben Pon's idea, and Heinz Nordhoff's faith in it, had certainly paid off; Volkswagen Type 2 Transporters were a familiar sight not only in their native Germany but throughout the world.

For 1962, a high-top Transporter offering 212 cubic feet (6 cubic metres) of load space was added to the range, and proved an immediate hit. The front indicator pods were replaced with large amber discs in 1963, and

In Denmark the Bus is known as the "Loaf." (Split-window Panel van).

In Germany the Bus became known affectionately as the "Bulli" - it does have a bulldog-like mien. (1966 Split-window).

Initially, the Bus was furnished with a very small back window - but who cares when the rear shelf is packed to the roof anyway?

Opposite - A Type 2 Pick-up was a rugged and dependable workhorse: it was also available with a wider bed. This Pick-up sports American-style bumpers. (1965).

The VW prepares to scale new heights.

an amber segment was added to the rear cluster, too. For 1963, a new engine (from the Type 3) of 1497cc, which delivered 42bhp, was introduced. In this guise the Transporter also sported upgraded brakes and suspension. The two engine types would be offered as options for just over a year before the less powerful unit was withdrawn.

In 1964 sliding side doors became an option and the size of the road wheels was reduced again. The pull-out door handles were replaced with the push-button variety, as was the T-bar of the rear

hatch. The tailgate was made wider and fitted with a torsion strut to support it when open. As a result of the increase in the tailgate's width, a larger rear window was incorporated. The louvred air intake slots above the rear wheelarches were also changed; previously they had faced outwards (like a cheese grater), and now they faced in.

In 1966 the tailgate handle was changed again, and a column-mounted dip-switch replaced the previous foot-switch. Despite the sales figures, which might well have

suggested the perfect product, there was a general dislike among customers of the 6-volt electrical system. In 1967, it was finally jettisoned in favour of a 12-volt system.

For "Splittie" fanatics, the outlook was not so bright ... Volkswagen had a new model planned to replace the old Transporter so the Split-screen was about to take a final bow. The last Split-screen Type 2 was built in July 1967, with 1.8 million having been produced, in total, during just over seventeen years of production life.

BAY-WINDOWS & WEDGES

1967 represented a major milestone in the history of the Volkswagen company. Dr. Heinz Nordhoff had been in failing health for a couple of years, and had already taken the decision that he would soon retire. His successor was to be Dr. Kurt Lotz, a well-respected industrialist who made it clear from his first speeches and press briefings in June of that year that he was going to uphold the traditions of Dr. Nordhoff. By the time that the new Transporters were introduced in August, Dr. Nordhoff was seriously ill, and Dr. Lotz took over the running of the company. Dr. Heinz Nordhoff died on the 12th April 1968, at the age of 69.

Although the introduction of the one-piece windscreen ("Bay Window" - as they would be popularly termed) Transporters in place of the split windscreen models marked the end of an era, the new breed was well-received. This version's 'face' was different, but it had character, was bright, cleanly modern and was still Bus-shaped. The new model was 10cm longer than the original, and there was a

great deal more space in the cab area, as well as in the rear - which had a load capacity of 177 cubic feet (5 cubic metres). The one-piece, curved windscreen gave excellent forward visibility, and a larger rear window improved the rear view, too. Below the windscreen was a strip of louvres for cab ventilation; the indicators were positioned just above the bumper, which curved around the van corners and incorporated a much-welcomed step at each end to make getting in and out of the cab easier. The new model was fitted with a different engine - again, courtesy of the Type 3 - a 1584cc unit that produced 47bhp and gave the Bus a top speed of around 65mph (110kph). Other improvements included new double-jointed swing axles, which improved the handling no end, wider track, and dual-circuit braking. Sliding loading doors were now standard, and there was a whole host of optional extras to choose from when ordering your new Type 2.

The Bay Window Bus came in the same body options as its predecessor - Panel van,

This Transporter was originally owned by the proprietor of a Belgian cheese shop. On one side the signwriting is in Flemish and on the other side in French - no point in losing customers by getting the language wrong! (Bay-window Panel van).

It was possible to order sliding doors on both sides of the van for ease of loading.

Kombi, Microbus (its special version now called the Clipper), Pick-up, Double Crew Cab and High-top (which, from 1968, had its upper section made of fibreglass).

In 1969 the rigidity of the body was increased, the doors were strengthened and a collapsible steering column was fitted as standard. The following year saw engine power increased to 50bhp and disc brakes replaced drums at the front. Cosmetically, there was little change, but the famous domed hubcaps were replaced by less-exciting flat ones. The three millionth Transporter milestone was passed in this year, too.

New for 1971 was a larger engine option - the 1679cc unit from the Type 4. This gave

A VW Camper can be quite a home from home.

The Type 2 is a proven favourite amongst those into watersports and the beach lifestyle.

The Bay Window VWs came in much the same varieties as the Split-screen, and the Microbus was a very popular one.

the bus power to its elbow to the tune of 66bhp, and increased the top speed to 77mph (125kph). 1971 also brought larger rear light clusters, the moving of the fuel filler further back so that it was reachable with the sliding door open, and an improvement in soundproofing. In 1972 an innovative crumple zone was introduced for safety, and the following year the cab step was redesigned so that it was indoors rather than out! Another, relatively small, change that year made a big difference to the look of the front; the indicators moved up to the ends of the air-intake grille.

In 1973, the Transporter said goodbye to the 1679cc engine and hello to a 1795cc unit giving even more power - 68bhp - and an even greater top speed of around 80mph (130kph). The downside was that the fuel consumption -

A Bus basks on a Cornish beach during the annual British "Run to the Sun" Volkswagen meeting. (1977 Bay-window Devon camper).

Some paint-jobs are more idiosyncratic than others ... (1973 Bay-window Panel van).

VW Clubs, of which there are a great number, take their Transporters just as seriously as their Beetles.

The Wedge Transporters replaced the Bays in 1979; less curves, more angles - as emphasised by this customised Pick-up.

Hanging out with a VW ...

always reckoned to hover around the 25/27mpg mark - dropped to the low twenties.

There was little further change until late 1975, when yet more power - 70bhp this time - was endowed upon the Bus by a new 1970cc engine. The following year brought redesigned door handles with safety in mind, and seatbelt mountings all round. There was an automatic option available, too. The Caravelle, an eight-seater special edition of the Microbus, arrived in 1978, and it turned out to be the last innovation of the Bay Window era. The following year, a new model was announced to replace the Bay.

The Double-cab Pick-up version of the Wedge; the six-seater cab made it ideal for teams of workers needing to move both materials and themselves. Lowering, alloys and dark glass make this particular wedge a mean machine.

The new model was much
more angular, supposedly
more aerodynamic, certainly
more modern - futuristic even,
considering that this was 1979.
The same basic body options
were still on offer, all tried and
tested over thirty years of
production. The new shape
was 12cm wider than the old,
and the windscreen, which
sloped steeply back, was
much larger. Below the lead-
ing point of the nose was a
grille of full width, framing both
headlamps and a VW roundel
(much smaller than before),
while the indicators moved
back down to just above
bumper level. Rear illumina-
tion incorporated modern
light clusters with integral fog
and reversing lamps. The rear
window was huge, and the
tailgate opened easily with
the aid of gas-filled struts.
There was a big increase in
space inside and the loading
height had been reduced by
around 13cm (the engine
being accessed by lifting a
hatch in the rear compartment). There was a choice of
engine - 1584cc or 1970cc,
again with an automatic
option on the latter. One of
the major modifications was
the introduction of coil-spring
suspension to replace the old
torsion-bar system.

There were not to be many
changes during the short
production life of the
"Wedge" - as it became
known. In 1980, a diesel-
engined, water-cooled,
version of the Transporter was

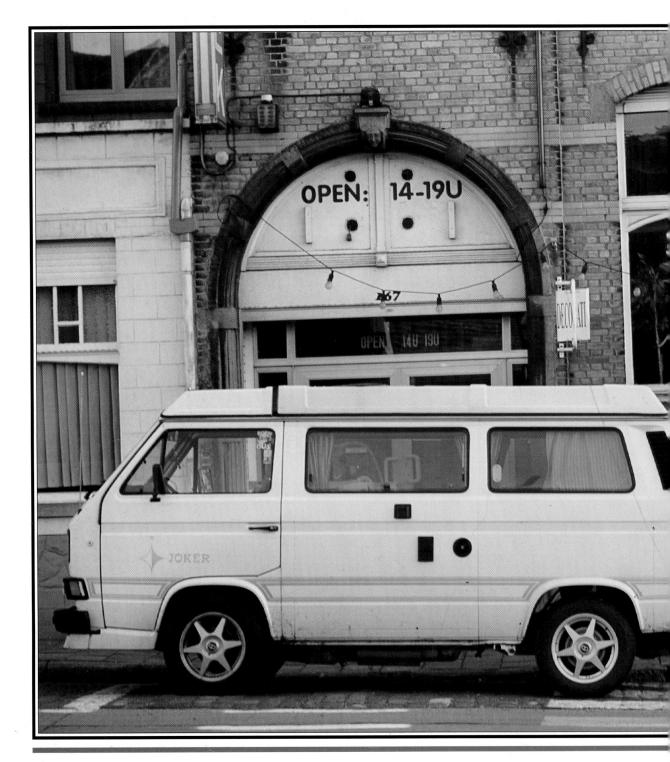

There was an even greater amount of space available inside the Wedge VWs.

produced its conventional four cylinder engine taken from the Golf/Rabbit model which was followed, in 1983, by a water-cooled flat-four *Wasserboxer*.

In 1982 a Caravelle version of the Bus was launched, with a luxuriously comfortable, no expense spared interior.

That the air-cooled Wedge was built for only four years is no reflection on either the model's abilities or its popularity, but times were changing and technology was moving on apace. The air-cooled philosophy that had first made Volkswagen's name with the Beetle was lagging behind in the race for more power and quietness. The last rear-engined, air-cooled Transporter rolled off the production line on the last day of 1982 - marking the end of a thirty-three year production run, during which an incredible 4.8 million units had been manufactured.

"The Joker" - a statuesque Wedge-based camper.

IN PUBLIC SERVICE

It was hardly surprising that Volkswagen would be approached to build vehicles for both the emergency services and the public utilities. They already had the perfect vehicle in the Transporter, with its big and unfussy interior and ready-made range of body options.

In 1952, VW started producing an ambulance based on the Kombi. Standard equipment in the basic ambulance included a heating system which, after driving just a few yards, started heating the interior. The heating was fully adjustable and could be used in conjunction with the electric fresh air ventilator built into the roof. A dividing window with a sliding panel separated cab and ambulance compartment; a roller blind was fitted to darken the interior. Two stretchers and a portable chair for patients, plus a doctor's chair and nurse's chair, were supplied and, for the very small patient, a socket to take an incubator connection was installed. There were cupboards for instruments, bandages and the portable first aid kit, pockets for splints and a hook for

the plasma bottle. If the patient was travelling alone in the rear he could summon attention from the other side of the glass by means of a buzzer near the stretcher.

The front of the ambulance had an illuminated sign on the roof. A spotlight was fitted to the centre of the windscreen, and the four indicator lights could be used like modern hazard warning lights. Extras that could be ordered included a two-tone horn, flashing roof-light and foglamps. Of course, there was also a deal of specialised equipment that could be ordered and fitted at the customer's request to suit particular applications. Some ambulances were for use as emergency response vehicles, some for comfortable and safe transport of the elderly and infirm and others for Red Cross work.

The Bus was ideal as an ambulance because it was neither too large nor too small, was affordable and reasonably inexpensive to run and, being air-cooled, would tend to keep going when other vehicles froze up or overheated. In short, it was reliable

VW ambulances were in demand from the Red Cross, as well as hospitals and clinics throughout the world. (Split-window ambulance).

- the primary requisite for any emergency vehicle.

Reliability was also the reason the Bus became renowned for its suitability as a fire-engine. Small towns, in charge of their own fire-fighting facilities, found a VW fitted the bill when budgeting and did not let them down in service. Base transporters - usually vans or pick-ups - were supplied by Volkswagen to specialist firms to kit out with the necessary fire-fighting equipment; one of the most well-known of these specialists was Magirus, based in Ulm.

Transporters were also popular with police forces, the German Post Office, who also purchased a large number of Beetles, and the German Forestry Departments. They made ideal hearses, of either the plain or highly embellished variety, too. There seems to have been a Transporter to cope with every one of life's journeys!

There was even a VW Schoolbus, based on the Kombi, which was, without doubt, designed by someone with first-hand experience of schoolchildren. According to

the advertising literature the interior was robust and re-markably solid and - this is the clincher - absolutely every part of the inside was wash-able! The seating comprised a double and single bench seat with room for school bags, too.

Transporters turned up in a host of other useful guises; refrigerated vans, tipper trucks, mobile shops, glass-carriers, snowploughs and generator trucks, to name but a few. Versatility was the key to the Transporter's success.

This ambulance was originally owned by a quarry-working company; it was essential to have it on standby but, fortunately, it got very little use. When sold it was still in excellent condition. Inset - The roomy interior made life comfortable for the patient and the nurses. (Original Split-window ambulance).

Present-day owner of this superb VW ambulance, Dirk Grobben, has kept the fittings intact and added period accessories, too.

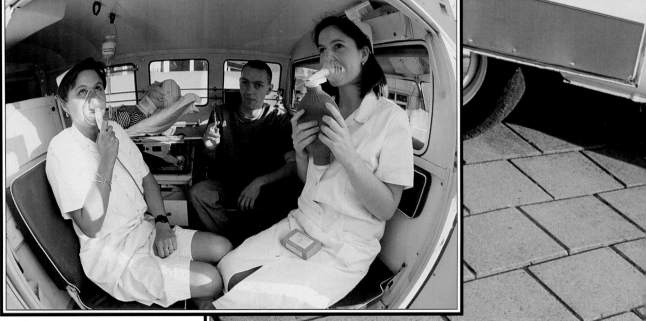

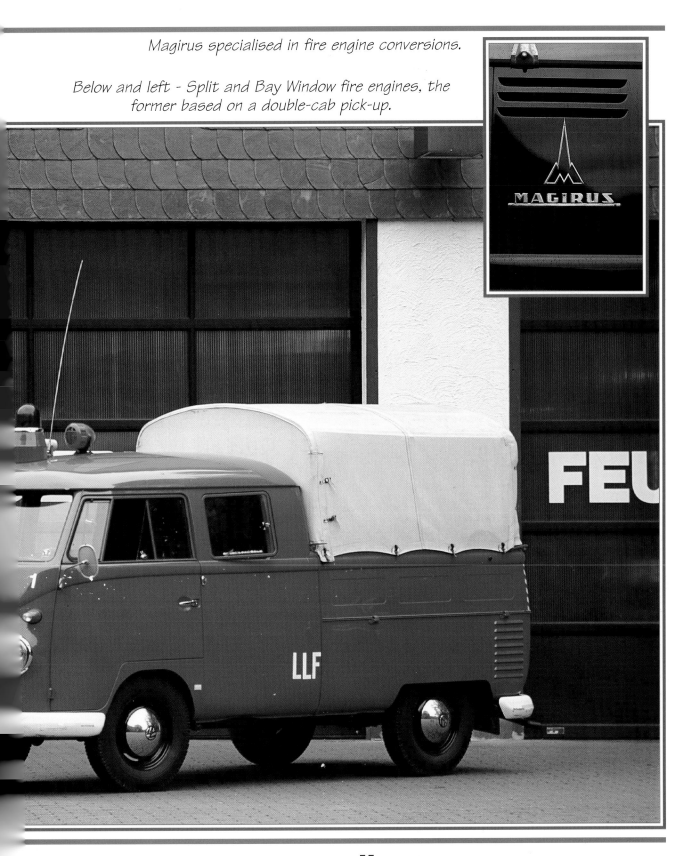

Magirus specialised in fire engine conversions.

Below and left - Split and Bay Window fire engines, the former based on a double-cab pick-up.

A Wedge-based fire engine,
in this case designed and
kitted out by the Altenahr
Fire Department.

The Cristal brewery in Alken,
Belgium, owns its own on-
site Split-window VW fire
engine.

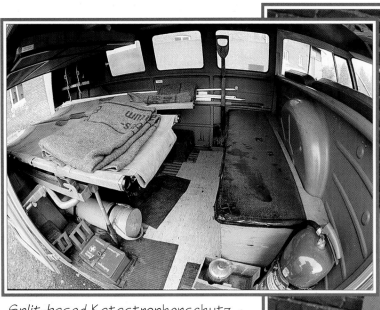

Split-based Katastrophenschutz -
a disaster response vehicle from
Rheinland Pfalz; equipped with
ladders and floodlamps, stretchers,
first aid equipment, digging and
cutting gear.

The Transporter as a hearse - sober and dignified with a plain, tasteful cross on the side.

Opposite - This slightly more decorative hearse was one of ten manufactured by Pollmann of Bremen and dates from 1965. It is 60cm longer (23.6in) and 20cm (7.9in) higher than the standard bus.

Not a cleverly manipulated VW logo, but the trademark of undertakers Mathaus Vogel, original owners of this hearse.

CAMPERS 5

In the austere days that followed the end of the war, the average person had little enough money for necessities, let alone for luxuries such as holidays. By the early 'fifties, things began to improve, but spending money on expensive hotels was out of the question for ordinary people, especially for families supporting small children.

VW realised that they had, in the Type 2, the answer to this problem; the Bus would make an ideal camping van. The box-shape was ideal for kitting out with camping gear, it had none of the power/weight/parking problems of the cumbersome car-towing-caravan combination and it was affordable. Once fitted out, it could be used as day-to-day transport too, with the advantage over a car of its diverse load-carrying ability.

Volkswagen were understandably very careful when searching for a company to build the Campervans that would carry the VW name. As with the choice of Karmann to build the convertible Beetle, Volkswagen looked for a well-established firm with a good reputation - and found

Westfalia. Volkswagen's literature for the Westfalia pushed home the message from the start. "Adventure with comfort? Yes, it's here at last, and no longer just for arm-chair travellers. No need to dream in vain of far horizons while booking the family for the nearest overcrowded holiday resort. The VW Camper has brought the comfortable, yet unconventional holiday within your reach."

Westfalia had its origins in the blacksmith's forge started by Johan Knobel in the mid-19th century. He began by making agricultural machinery and, by the time his sons, Franz and Wilhelm, took over the reins, the company was actively involved in making horse-drawn carriages. As this market dried up with the increased popularity of carriages of the horseless variety, the family-run company moved into other areas, including trailers and caravans. They had a fine reputation for quality of materials and craftsmanship, employing over 250 craftsmen by the end of the 1930s. Then came the war and the destruction of so

The firms of Volkswagen and Westfalia enjoyed a long and successful business relationship based on the fitting out of Transporters as campers. (US-spec Bay-window camper from 1978).

Transporter camping can be whatever you want - from practical and functional to luxurious. Both these conversions were built by Westfalia.

many factories - Westfalia fared no better than Volkswagen, and found themselves starting from scratch when peace returned. They made quick progress and by 1947 were exhibiting their first caravan made of steel plate, and were soon in negotiations with Volkswagen about a joint project - a campervan based on VW's new commercial vehicle.

The first VW Westfalia appeared in 1951; it was an instant hit, and production began in earnest. Standard fitments included berths for

Living/dining room becomes a bedroom in a matter of moments in this entirely original Westfalia camper.

Isabella is happy to pose outside friend Erik's Bay-window, high-top, camper conversion. The Swiss Post Office owned it before Erik and it's right hand drive so that the postman could get out onto the pavement, not into the traffic. (Isabella is a little VW-crazy!)

This VW started life as a Magirus fire-truck, but now it's a camper with the exterior colour scheme carried through inside; note the bright red sink!

two adults and one/two children, a pop-up top with ventilation windows, a sink and cooker unit, fridge, tables, lights and curtains. Options available included stand-alone awning, roof-rack with ladder and extra cupboards.

Westfalias were very popular in the USA and, at a time when the European Tour was becoming a favoured American holiday, Volkswagen offered a service whereby a Westfalia could be ordered to one's specification in the USA and picked up on arrival in Germany. The service included advice on touring, servicing and the logistics of taking the van back home to the States. The profitable working relationship between VW and Westfalia lasted

FREIWILLIGE FEUERWEHR
RAHMS/STRAUSCHEID

SI · MK 825

throughout the production life of the Type 2 with over 250,000 Westfalia campers built in all.

In the UK there were several popular makes of camper based on the Transporter. Devon Campers, which were built by the J P White company of Sidmouth - in Devon - came in several different levels of trim, the most popular being the Microbus-based Caravette, with sleeping accommodation for two adults and two children. The Dormobile, whose name became a generic term for any camping van in the UK, was fitted out by the Martin Walter Company. It had a cleverly-designed roof which was side-elevating, with extra sleeping accommodation incorporated. Danbury Conversions used mainly panel vans for their conversions, fitting their own design of windows. Their interior fittings were adaptable and removable; Danburys could easily lead multiple lives as business vehicles and people carriers, reverting to camper form for weekends and holidays. Of course, there are a huge number of unique VW Campers around, their style and scope limited only by the priorities and abilities of their owners/convertors. Panel vans, Kombis, firetrucks, ambulances, even a former hearse, have been pressed into use as campers: one started life as a Pick-up.

Kemperink conversions from the Netherlands were primarily intended as commercial vehicles, having their wheelbase extended by over

Clever British Dormobile conversion has side-elevating roof, rear kitchen unit and seats that can be easily re-arranged or removed, giving spacious and versatile accomodation. Note the spare wheel housing behind the front seats. (Split-window 1964).

The long-wheelbase Kemperink makes an ideal camper conversion because of the space it offers; this one carries all the essentials for a good weekend!

Not everyone's camping priorities are the same; the keyword is versatility - something the Transporter knows all about. Marc and Martine Plaetsier with their much-travelled and much-loved camper. (1968 Bay-window).

a metre, and kitted out for jobs such as mobile chip shops and ice-cream vans but, with their extra length and height, they make first-rate campers!

For Marc and Martine Plaetsier, their affair with the VW Bus began when they bought a battered old specimen from a drinks store in Johannesburg. Initially they used it to travel all over southern Africa and, as they warmed to its charms, the idea of a much longer trek with their bus started to crystalise. They re-registered the bus in Swaziland, got new passports for themselves - South African registrations and passport stamps were bad news at that time - and set off. They travelled north through Botswana, Zambia, Malawi, Uganda, Tanzania and Kenya. They were struck by the contrasts - the difficult and hazardous life of Amin's Uganda, the breathtaking beauty of the Kenyan wildlife reserves.

From Kenya they took a boat to India - a thirteen-day journey during which the boat broke down several times. After several months touring, the bus broke down too - mainly due to Indian (72 octane) petrol - in a remote village. Helped by an audi-

ence of around 200, some of whom had travelled from nearby villages to watch, they dismantled the engine, which had been severely damaged by a broken valve. The damaged parts were packed into a rucksack; there was nothing for it but to hitch a ride to Delhi, and the nearest VW agency, 400 kilometres (250 miles) away. After three days in the city, and with help from the German Embassy staff there, they had found everything they needed and hitched back to the village. They could not believe what they saw; the rest of the engine, along with all the nuts

and bolts, had vanished ... Where did they go from here - and how? They decided to sleep on the problem and, in the morning, a local man appeared with the engine pieces; fearing they would be stolen, he'd taken everything to his house for safe-keeping. Thanks to their good samaritan, Marc and Martine were soon on their way again.

After India came Sikim, Nepal, Pakistan and Afghanistan - where the VW was 'strip-searched' for drugs so thoroughly that it took two days to put everything back together again. Then on to Iran, where the bus skidded on an icy mountain pass, coming to rest with one back wheel over the edge of a ravine. Fortunately an ancient passing truck came to their rescue and pulled them to the safety of the road. The rest of the trip, through Turkey, Greece, Yugoslavia, Austria, Germany and back home to Belgium, went quite smoothly! The Plaetsiers still own their bus. They say they fell in love with it the very first time they drove in it and, as the three of them have been through a lot together, they have no intention of ever parting with it.

STRANGE TRANSPORTERS

Not all one-offs are cosmetic customisations or campers. Some are workmanlike, and some are strange ...

Transporters cope with most ordinary road conditions admirably but, in 1962, a Viennese firm decided to create a Bus that would definitely be unfazed by "snow, sand, stones, alpine meadows, moors, streams or woods." This was no ordinary Bus; two wheels at the front - on each side - another set of four behind that and, at the rear, a set of half-tracks! A formidable beast that would be "... an ideal helper for everyone - landlord, hunter, forester, doctor, maintenance personnel for ski-lifts, television, radio, pipelines and so on." - or, at least, that's what the manufacturer's promotional material said.

Another VW curiosity, at first glance, the *Brandstofcellenwagen* looks just like any other Type 2 Panel van, in fact, it's a unique experimental VW and part of the search for cleaner, cheaper, safer, renewable fuels which has gone on since

someone first suggested that using fossil fuels to power vehicles might not be such a good idea after all.

Up closer, complex-looking equipment can be glimpsed through the windows, but it's only when the doors are opened that this VW's secrets come to light. The *Brandstofcellenwagen* is packed to the roof with strange-looking equipment - twelve electrolytic cells provide power to the Siemens electric motor which powers the Bus. The system necessitates twelve large batteries - which slide out on trays - and twelve cylinders of hydrogen gas, as well as some highly complex electronic switching and monitoring equipment. The result is one very heavy Bus!

The VW Bus made its mark by being versatile. Whether in the shape of van, pick-up, camper, people carrier - or one of its more specialised or eccentric forms - its popularity never wanes. The VW Bus will be with us for a long time to come ...

One of the strangest things you could do to a Transporter? In fact, the concept of fitting half-tracks makes sense - here's a vehicle that can cope with the conditions of the Austrian Alps in all weathers. The idea was not totally new, as some wartime versions of the Beetle-derived Kubelwagen were fitted with half-tracks, too. (Based on 1962 Split-window Kombi).

The Brandstofcellenwagen looks quite ordinary from the outside.

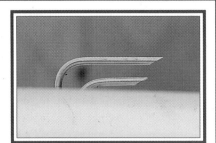

The process gives off vapour, which escapes through these futuristic outlets in the roof.

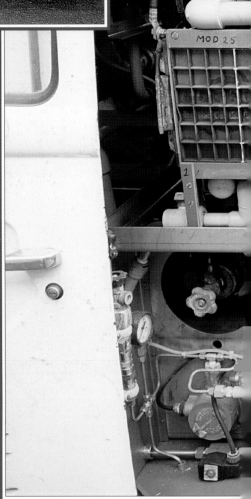

You can see four of the twelve cells, with hydrogen cylinders underneath. Beneath the green floor are twelve car-size batteries.

61·49·UB

Transporters were
converted for many
different commercial uses -
in high-top mode they made
ideal fast-food outlets.

In the mid-'sixties, a small
quantity of Transporters
were fitted out for the
military authorities of the
Netherlands for use as
radio cars. The Pick-up
(pages 82 & 83) started
life as one of these radio
cars, but is now in everyday
civilian use.

A very useful addition to local authority fleets; a turntable ladder-equipped Pick-up scales new heights and saves time!
(1971 Bay-window Pick-up).

Proving there's nothing new under the sun - a delivery van for "Florida Boy Orange" promotes the product with a period piece of advertising.

The VW Bus has always been great for customising to suit personal taste, a fashion that shows no sign of abating because of the Type 2's universal youthful appeal, longevity and availability.

GALLERY 7

Kultur-u.Lehrfilm-Instit
Klemens Lindenau

Split-window Kombi.

Split-window Firetruck.

94

Dear Reader,
We hope you enjoyed this Veloce Publishing production. If you have ideas for other books on VW, or other marques, please write and tell us.
Meantime, Happy Motoring!

There are also Veloce Colour Family Albums on Bubblecars & Microcars (two), Vespa, Lambretta, VW Beetle, Citroen DS, Citroen 2CV and Mini and Mini Cooper. More titles are in preparation.

Photographer's postscript

The trusty R6 Leicas I have worked with for many years continued to deliver the goods until one cold and wet November morning when I was in the middle of photographing Christian Birkholz's hearse in Ingolstadt, Bavaria. It was the sort of rain and the sort of wind that indoors was made for and, to be out in it, especially on some exposed bleak hill, bordered on the wrong side of misery. Having travelled to the location in the aforementioned hearse didn't help, although the company was alive and convivial.

Twenty minutes into this numbing shoot, my camera simply jammed. I reached for the spare and put a film in it, only to discover that in the process the film had got so wet it stuck to the pressure plate, making film advance impossible. Back in the hearse I dried everything out and loaded another, drier film. The shoot

continued and, despite everything, it went very well. (On my return to the UK, Leica diagnosed and repaired a broken spring!) Christian and his girlfriend, Iris, were most hospitable, and sent me off full of hot white sausages - a speciality of the area.

I mention this event not because it is desperately important, but to illustrate a simple point; even the very best equipment can fail (and it's never when you're at home) but the way in which the manufacturer deals with the problem is how you discover the real meaning of quality. I am pleased to report that Leica in Milton Keynes were charming and efficient.

The same can be said for the many Type 2 owners who were kind enough to allow me to photograph their vehicles - some of them waited around for hours - and, in some instances, put me up overnight. I will not repeat the whole 'thanks' page,

but I must again thank Mon & Cory Martens, the eccentric Raoul Verbeemen and Dirk Grobben, not forgetting the charming 'nurses' in the shapes of Ilse and Dinny - true stars! For those who read the *VW Beetle Colour Family Album*, I must report that the coffee at Etienne Mertens' is as good as ever.

The Bullikartei were kind enough to invite me to their meeting in Altenahr and Jochen and Roswitha Brauer put me up later in the year while I photographed the most interesting half-track. We talked late into the night and, during the conversation, Roswitha mentioned a science fiction strip cartoon that was around in the States at the time certain Bullis were being built in Europe. "I think," she said with charm and authority, "it was called 'Gordon Flash.'" Magic!

David Sparrow